CONTENTS

DEDICATION 5
ACKNOWLEDGEMENT 7
INTRODUCTION 9
CHAPTER 1 16
CHAPTER 2 36
CHAPTER 3 73
CHAPTER 4 95
CHAPTER 5 136
CHAPTER 6 168
CHAPTER 7 187

ISBN: 978 – 9988 – 2 – 9053 – 5
Copyright © 2019, FOSTER ANTWI

Scripture Literate Evangelical Ministry

Call for further explanation, counselling, and prayers. God richly bless you!!!

Contact: +233 (0)265 62 92 65
Whatsapp: +233 (0)543 48 22 49
Email: antwifoster95@yahoo.com

SPIRITUAL CODE OF POWER

PUBLISHED By: Christ's Vessel
Publishing House,
P. O. BOX 1820, Koforidua,
Ghana, West Africa
Tel: +233 543 482 249 /
       +233 265 629 265

<u>AUTHOR</u>

EVANGELIST FOSTER ANTWI
(REVEREND MINISTER)

DEDICATION

This book is specially dedicated to my former and current employers.

My former employer, Mr. William Osei-Darko, the Director of Prince of Peace Schools, Adweso Koforidua, and his wife, Mrs. Deborah Asare Nortei, for their love, care and diverse contributions to my life. I'm eternally grateful to them for the foundation they laid for me has helped me succeed in life. I am really proud of them. May God continue to bless them and enlarge their portions in Jesus'

Mighty name, Amen!

Moreover, I dedicate this book also to my present employer, Lady Miriam Ofosu Appiah, the Directoress of St. Mary's Day Care and Preparatory School, one of the outstanding ultra-modern private schools in Ghana located in Koforidua and Okorase. She is very prayerful, kind, humble, and a woman with grace worthy of emulation. She is more than a mother to me, my inspiration. May God continue to grant you a different, well-disciplined and results-oriented School. God richly bless you!

ACKNOWLEDGEMENT

I am eternally grateful to Jehovah God for His Spirit at work in me (1 John 2:27).

Having an idea and turning it into a book is not an easy task. The experience is both internally challenging and rewarding.

I especially want to thank Apostle Stephen Avoyam, the Principal and Director of Elyon Bible College-Ghana. Apostle, may God bless you and continue to use you to impart sound Biblical knowledge and to ordain His servants into the work of ministry.

Also, I want to thank my dearest friend, Hagan Amonuwaa Adorcia, for helping me throughout the drafting process to the completion of this book.

May God richly bless you!

INTRODUCTION

We are in a new era of our Christian life. God has blessed His ministers with profound insight into His word. Where we are now in God is no longer "Ask, and it will be given you; seek, and you will find; knock, and it will be opened to you." – Matthew 7:7RSV. It is no longer, **it will be given**, **you will find** and **it will be opened**. God has already solved that. Remember, Jesus spoke these words before the Holy Spirit descended upon the

Disciples to make His permanent abode in them. How do we ask, seek and knock? The answer is through prayer and meditation on the word of God. We can't ask, seek and knock enough for we do not even know how to pray unless the Spirit of God makes intercessions for us.

Jesus died for us and has freely given us His Spirit. According to the Word of God, He (God) has blessed us with all the blessings in the heavenly places.

He has made us accepted in the Beloved and has given unto us all that pertain to life and godliness (Ephesians 1:3-7). He is not thinking about it to make a decision. He's already done it!

1 Corinthians 2:9-16KJV, *"But as it is written, eye hath not seen, nor ear heard, neither have entered into the heart of man, the things which God hath prepared for them that love him.* **But God hath revealed them unto us by his Spirit: for the Spirit searcheth all things, yea, the deep things of God.** *For what man knoweth*

the things of a man, save the spirit of man which is in him? Even so the things of God knoweth no man, but the Spirit of God. **Now we have received, not the spirit of the world, but the spirit which is of God; that we might know the things that are freely given to us of God.** *Which things also we speak, not in the words which man's wisdom teacheth, but which the Holy Ghost teacheth; comparing spiritual things with spiritual. But the natural man receiveth not the things of the Spirit of God: for they are foolishness unto him: neither can he know them, because they are spiritually* *discerned. But he that is spiritual judgeth all things, yet he himself is judged of no man. For who hath known the mind of the Lord, that he may instruct him? But **we have the mind of Christ**."*

Whatever would cause us to ask, seek and knock has already been taken care of by the Spirit of God at work in us. We only have to manifest what God says about us by our daily confessions.

God is causing a dynamic change in our knowledge of Him and our confessions as pastors. No longer will pastors shout, **TAKE IT, RECEIVE IT, GOD WILL VISIT YOU**, and so on during ministrations.

No longer will the body of Christ raise their hands high up in the air and expect the power of God from the heavens to fall on them. Never again will church members wrestle to receive a touch from the man of God before they realize God has visited them. This has been the thought of many Christians.

The truth is that God is not a visitor who visits for a short period of time and goes back to where he came. Instead, God has made His abode in us. We are in Him and He is in us. We are simply one with him. Hallelujah!

CHAPTER 1

Speak According to Revelation

"Satanic altars, horns, generational curses, faulty foundations, and un-healthy soul ties have power on those Christians with identity crises who are glued to such elementary teachings. They are those who refuse to grow in the things of God, infants feeding on breast milk. Hear me, there is absolutely nothing greater and powerful than the Spirit

of God in us which brings liberation. The Christian is God's army commander on earth. No army commander who thinks himself as a vulnerable infant feeding on breast milk can ever win a war at the spiritual battlefront. The war front is not for crying babies, it is for the mature in Christ, those who have discovered their identity and are able to talk according to the revelation of the Word of God." – Rev. Foster Antwi

2 Corinthians 6:10KJV, "As sorrowful, yet always rejoicing; as poor, yet

making many rich; as having nothing,
and yet possessing all things."

*1 Corinthians 3:21KJV, "Therefore let no man glory in men. **For all things are yours."***

*1 John 2:20KJV, "But **ye have an unction from the Holy One, and ye know all things."***

Shout I receive it! Receive it! Take it! Are some of the words we mostly hear proclaim by ministers of the Gospel. The question then is, what is it that the children of God should receive? It is the restoration of their health, financial breakthrough, marriage, fruit of the womb, safe delivery, travelling, business opportunities, promotions at work place, scholarship, success, favour, grace, the list goes on and on.

But have you ever paused for a second to reflect on these proclamations to find out whether they are in line with Bible doctrine particularly the revelation of the new creation man created by the word of God?

Maybe you might think they are words of faith spoken by the Man of God, but as you take time to learn in this book, you would come to have a different perception which would catapult you to another level and dimension of your Christian walk where you would start to experience the divinity in you in a way you've not experienced before.

Let's look at what happens when our confessions are in variance with the revelation of who we've become in Christ. To start with, some members of the Body of Christ begin to expect some external force to come upon them. They begin to look outside of themselves and with great expectations, hope to be touched by the Spirit of God.

Again, in their minds and heart, not only do they yearn to receive, but then they begin to visualize themselves being touched by some kind of divine hand and the result is that, they fall not by the Spirit of God, but by the power of their own imagination. These things easily open doors for demonic manipulations and all kinds of false healings and deliverance.

There is another great danger! In today's churches, some members attend services in the name of a particular Man of God. Members struggle to touch the man of God or use all kinds of mechanisms to catch the attention of the man of God to minister to them simply because they feel they lack something. I mean, their attention and faith is solely based on that particular minister known to have some extraordinary anointing to break yokes. They lose focus of the reality that, it is Jesus Christ at work in the man of God and the miracles that the man of God perform are not by himself, but by the leading and guidance of the Holy Spirit if truly he is of God.

Those who lack this basic understanding substitute the presence of Jesus Christ in the midst of the saints for ONLY the physical appearance of the Man of God. The man of God is seen as the only person with the divine nature in him. This is not the case dearest reader. The Holy Spirit is in all of us, we are His abode and we all carry God inside of us. We are all the anointed of God in the Body of Christ. It isn't like that village where the fetish priest is the only powerful entity consulted by all. Ignorance of this truth explains why many get disappointed when they are not ministered to by the man of God. Often, such people even feel reluctant to give their offerings to God. People are simply ready to give more only on condition that they receive a touch or prophecy from the minister.

It isn't only the members of the Body of Christ that sometimes get disappointed, but then most of the miracle pastors too get disappointed. When they expect a massive outpouring of the Holy Spirit and greater works done by God and they don't happen like that, they get disappointed and begin to think about what the members will say about them.

Some Prophets and ministers have turned into occultism all because of the lack of sound Biblical knowledge and partly because they want to prove they also have power and that God is using them too. The end is disastrous as you know already child of God.

Nowadays, demonstration of the power of God has become a competition among ministers of God that elders and other church leaders search diligently for a man of God known to have the ability to work more signs and wonders and invite those only to minister in their churches to help raise funds to complete some stand-still projects or to raise enough funds to start a different venture. What's happening is that most elders and leaders in the house of God lack certain basic revelations of the word of God. To tell you the truth, If John the Baptist was to be in our world today, he would never have been considered as an anointed Man of God with international acclaim by church elders and members alike because he didn't cast out devils, healed the sick or brought the dead back to life. Never decide who is anointed and who is not by the performance of signs and wonders dear reader. Let me show you how Jesus rated John the Baptist.

Matthew 11:7-11KJV, "7 And as they departed, Jesus began to say unto the multitudes concerning John, What went ye out into the wilderness to see? A reed shaken with the wind? But what went ye out for to see? A man clothed in soft raiment? behold, they that wear soft clothing are in kings' houses. But what went ye out for to see? A prophet? yea, I say unto you, and more than a prophet. For this is he, of whom it is written, Behold, I send my messenger before thy face, which shall prepare thy way before thee. Verily I say unto you, Among them that are born of women there hath not risen a greater than John the Baptist: notwithstanding he that is least in the kingdom of heaven is greater than he. (Study 2 Timothy

4:2-5)

Ministers have knowledge on the *anointing upon* but not much understanding of the *anointing within.* Even those who claim to have deeper revelation on the *anointing within* still are glued to the *anointing upon* the reason they keep shouting and repeating, **TAKE IT! RECEIVE IT!**

The time has come for the church of God to wake up from her slumber and begin to speak words in sync with the revelation of the new creation man created by the Word.

We as ministers of the Gospel ought to learn harder so we won't open doorways for fallen angels and all kinds of religious spirits to possess innocent souls by our wrong confessions.

2 Timothy 2:15KJV, "Study to shew thyself approved unto God, a workman that needeth not to be ashamed, rightly dividing the word of truth."

1 Timothy 4:16KJV, "Take heed unto thyself, and unto the doctrine; continue in them: for in doing this thou shalt both save thyself, and them that hear thee."

We can pollute our spirit by our wrong confessions due to ignorance of the word of God. We have to understand that we don't come before God in prayers anymore. We are in God and He is in us. We, therefore, do not need God to open the heavens to receive our prayers. Some Christians are of the view that we enter into the spirit during worship and prayers. This is not what the Bible teaches. The Bible teaches that we live in the Spirit. We don't also become spiritual when we enter church. We are spiritual because we fellowship with God. Those who do not have this understanding live a double life. They behave differently in church like angels and when they are out of the church, they go worldly. This is the result of ignorance of the word of God. It is about time you studied the word of God to know what the Bible actually says about the new creation. We are the children of the covenant God made with Abraham. We are the outcome of that covenant, the complete evidence that God watched over his word to perform it. God is indeed the covenant-keeping God! We do not need to make any covenant with God again. That time is passed and gone. We have now entered into the rest of God and we live in His presence, hence the time for covenant has expired. Don't go to church with huge sums of money to make a covenant with God just to claim the promises of God or to cause God to minister to your needs. Those are ma-nipulative teachings and they only put you in bondage, it makes you a spiritual slave. Do not allow yourself to be manipulated by any of those elementary teachings I mentioned in the opening of this chapter for you were bought with a price (1 Corinthians 7:23). They will only enslave your soul in the end child of God. The time has come for you as a Christian to desist from any practice in the house of God that is not in consonant with the absolute Word of Truth. We need to study and teach souls to speak right, *"for by thy words thou shalt be justified, and by thy words thou shalt be condemned."- Matthew 12:37KJV*

I am confident that by the time you're done reading this book, you would declare as the Apostle Paul declared, *"I can do all things through Christ which strengtheneth me."- Philippians 4:13KJV*

CHAPTER 2

Be Conscious of the Power Within

"Anything that will not scare God must not scare you for you carry God's Spirit and you are one in spirit with God"- Rev. Foster Antwi

Ephesians 3:20KJV, "Now unto him that is able to do exceeding abundantly above *all that we ask or think, **according to the power that worketh in us**.*"

God is able to do more than we think according to His power working in us. Get to know, there is power inside of you.

*2 Timothy 1:7KJV, "For **God hath not given** us the spirit of fear; but of power, and of love, and of a sound mind."*

This also means that God has already deposited His Spirit in Us. The Spirit produces in us tremendous power, love and peace of mind.

*Luke 10:19KJV, "Behold, I give unto you power to tread on serpents and scorpions, **and over all the power of the enemy: and nothing shall by any means hurt you."***

We have been given power over the enemy. Be conscious of this truth child of God.

Colossians 1:8-22KJV, "Who also de-

clared unto us your love in the Spirit. For this cause we also, since the day we heard it, do not cease to pray for you, and to desire that ye might be filled with the knowledge of his will in all wisdom and spiritual understanding. That ye might walk worthy of the Lord unto all pleasing, being fruitful in every good work, and increasing in the knowledge of God; strengthened with all might, according to his glorious power, unto all patience and longsuffering with joyfulness; **giving thanks unto the Father, which hath made us meet to be partakers of the inheritance of the saints in light: who**

hath delivered us from the power of darkness, and hath translated us into the kingdom of his dear Son: In whom we have redemption through his blood, even the forgiveness of sins: who is the image of the invisible God, the firstborn of every creature: *for by him were all things created, that are in heaven, and that are in earth, visible and invisible, whether they be thrones, or dominions, or principalities, or powers: all things were created by him, and for him: And he is before all things, and by him all things consist. And he is the head of the body, the church: who is the beginning, the first-*

born from the dead; that in all things he might have the preeminence. For it pleased the Father that in him should all fullness dwell; And, having made peace through the blood of his cross, by him to reconcile all things unto himself; by him, I say, whether they be things in earth, or things in heaven. **And you, that were sometime alienated and enemies in your mind by wicked works, yet now hath he reconciled in the body of his flesh through death, to present you holy and unblameable and unreproveable in his sight:"**

Notice that we have been forgiven and are no longer enemies. God has already by His power delivered us from the power of Satan and has given us an inheritance. This gives us boldness to walk in dominion on earth.

God has bestowed enormous power within us. That power isn't dormant. You may not feel anything within, but it is at work in you. It is the working of the Spirit in us that confirms our son-ship. That same Spirit produces the ability to pray, attend church services and make us love fellow human beings with the same kind of love that God loves us. It works to make our natural spirit desire and focus only on things of the Spirit and not of the flesh.

That same Spirit produces faith in us the more we hear the word of God and causes us to be doers of the word and not just hearers. That Spirit is found in the word of God and it cuts through the spirit of man and convicts him of his sins to accept Christ.

Jesus knew what he carried. He was

conscious of the power in Him. He looked within and drew power to do the many signs and wonders. Jesus never accomplished anything by Himself. Rather, it was God doing the mighty works. Jesus was very sensitive to the Spirit and whatever he heard the father speak, that he also spoke.

John 14:10KJV, "Believest thou not that I am in the Father, and the Father in me? the words that I speak unto you I speak not of myself: but the Father that dwelleth in me, he doeth the works."

Jesus was God Himself in the flesh. He simply demonstrated to the disciples how they should live the life of the New Creation. The new creation doesn't look outside of himself to work the things of the Spirit. Instead, he looks within and draws power from the rivers of living water flowing from his spirit which is Christ in you the hope of glory.

John 7:38KJV, "He that believeth on me, as the scripture hath said, out of his belly shall flow rivers of living water."

The Holy Spirit comes to make his eternal abode in us the moment we believe in our hearts and confess the Lordship of Christ. The Holy Spirit doesn't come upon us for a short period of time and leave when His work is done in us as was witnessed in the Old Testament.

In the New Testament, God has cleansed us, sanctified us, declared us righteous and accepted us in the

Beloved not of our own works or deeds but according to the finished work of Jesus, His Son.

Titus 3:5KJV, "Not by works of righteousness which we have done, but according to his mercy he saved us, by the washing of regeneration, and renewing of the Holy Ghost."

1 Corinthians 6:9-11KJV, "Know ye not that the unrighteous shall not inherit the kingdom of God? Be not deceived: neither fornicators, nor idolaters, nor adulterers, nor effeminate, nor abusers of themselves with mankind, nor thieves, nor covetous, nor drunkards, nor revilers, nor extortioners, shall inherit the kingdom of God. And such were some of you; but ye are washed, but ye are sanctified, but ye are justified in the name of the Lord Jesus, and by the Spirit of our God."

Romans 8:29,30KJV, "For whom he did foreknow, he also did predestinate to be conformed to the image of his Son, that he might be the firstborn among many brethren. Moreover whom he did predestinate, them he also called: and whom he called, them he also justified: and whom he justified, them he also glorified."

God has therefore blessed us with His Holy Spirit. This same Holy Spirit is the anointing of God that lives in us. This anointing which we have received from God abides in us, teaches us all things that pertain to life and godliness and reveal unto us the deeper things of God.

1 John 2:27KJV, "But the anointing which ye have received of him abideth in you, and ye need not that any man teach you: but as the same anointing teacheth you of all things, and is truth, and is no lie, and even as it hath taught you, ye shall abide in him."

Paul understood the power working in us and boldly declared we are not ignorant of the devices of the enemy (2 Corinthians 2:11). This is so because, the Spirit in us reveals the minds and plots of Satan and his cohort of demons to us. Thank God we are always wiser than our enemies!

The power of God at work in us is the same power that raised Jesus Christ from the dead. That same power is able to quicken our mortal bodies. It can heal every disease and infirmity in our lives irrespective of the cause. This is to say that, God's power is greater than every sickness and infirmity ever discovered or yet to be discovered. It flows throughout every cell, tissue, fibre, bone, water, and blood in our bodies causing us to walk in divine health.

Romans 8:11KJV, "But if the Spirit of him that raised up Jesus from the dead dwell in you, he that raised up Christ from the dead shall also quicken your mortal bodies by his Spirit that dwelleth in you."

The reason some of us are still struggling with some diseases and infirmities is that we are not conscious of the fact that we carry the same power Jesus used to perform all the miracles recorded in the Bible. God has given us this power called the anointing without measure and it has no limit in its operation.

To limit the power in us means limiting the arm of God, but God cannot be limited. God is bigger than our problems. Nothing is greater than our God, therefore, there is nothing that can ever scare God. ***Anything that will not scare God must not scare you for you carry God's spirit and you are one in spirit with God.*** Greater is He who is in us than he who is in the world. The following scriptures talk about God's power. Meditate on them child of God:

By his power he stilled the sea…Behold, these are but the outskirts of his ways, and how small a whisper do we hear of him! But the thunder of his power who can understand? Job 26:14 ESV

He heals the brokenhearted and binds up their wounds. He determines the number of the stars; he gives to all of them their names. Great is our Lord, and abundant in power; his understanding is beyond measure. Psalm 147:3-5 ESV

God thunders wondrously with his voice; he does great things that we cannot comprehend. Job 37:5ESV

He loads the thick cloud with moisture; the clouds scatter his lightning. They

turn around and around by his guidance, to accomplish all that he commands them on the face of the habitable world. Whether for correction or for his land or for love, he causes it to happen.
Job 37:13ESV

I am the Lord, and there is no other, besides me there is no God; I equip you, though you do not know me, that people may know, from the rising of the sun and from the west, that there is none besides me; I am the Lord, and there is no other. I form light and create darkness; I make well-being and create calamity; I am the

Lord, who does all these things. Isaiah 45:5-7ESV

...he who is the blessed and only Sovereign, the King of kings and Lord of lords, who alone has immortality, who dwells in unapproachable light, whom no one has ever seen or can see. To him be honor and eternal dominion. Amen. I Timothy 6:15, 16ESV

For he was crucified in weakness, but lives by the power of God. For we also are weak in him, but in dealing with you we will live with him by the power of God. 2 Corinthians 13:4ESV

But Jesus looked at them and said, "With man this is impossible, but with God all things are possible." Matthew 19:26ESV

Once God has spoken; twice have I heard this: that power belongs to God, and that to you, O Lord, belongs steadfast love... Psalm 62:11,12ESV

Behold, I am the Lord, the God of all flesh. Is anything too hard for me? Jeremiah 32:27ESV

Our God, majestic in power, has made his abode in us, hence all that is required on our part is our consciousness of what God in His infinite wisdom has done for us. God's power is already at work in us. What is required of us is expressing our faith in it by our confessions to cause tremendous manifestations of this power. I would show you how in a moment.

You see, there are so many ministers of God who attribute power to speaking in tongues. Many are of the opinion that the surest way to activate God's Spirit in us is by speaking in tongues. I do not condemn speaking in tongues neither do I challenge the power that is manifest when one speaks in an un-

known tongue as the spirit gives utter-
ances.

In all of Scripture, Jesus our Saviour never spoke in tongues. He spoke in plain languages that were known to the people of His days and which were meaningful. This is to say that, it isn't speaking in tongues that put the tre-mendous power of God in us to work. The Bible doesn't say that at all. In-stead, it says that the Spirit is already at work in us. It is working in us!

Speaking in tongues neither activate

nor cause the power in us to become operative. The power within us is God Himself residing in us. God isn't a robotic machine that operates under specific commands. We don't activate God by speaking in tongues. Whether or not we speak in tongues, God is still at work in us. Speaking in tongues connect our human spirit to the enormous power of God in us making us more sensitive to the Spirit's guidance in our lives. *"For it is God which worketh in you both to will and to do of his good pleasure"- Philippians 2:13KJV.*

We are not super powerful when we speak in tongues neither do we become powerless when we don't speak in tongues. We are super powerful not because we speak in tongues often, but because greater is the one in us than the one in the world.

1 John 4:4KJV, "Ye are of God, little children, and have overcome them: because greater is he that is in you, than he that is in the world."

Speaking in tongues has its own place in God. All the other gifts of God including the speaking in tongues come about as a result of God's power functioning in us. Exercising our spirit is not limited to speaking in tongues, but rather it has to do with all things that have to do with God and His kingdom.

God's power at work in us produces a strong desire in us to do the things of God.

"For to be carnally minded is death; but to be spiritually minded is life and peace."- Romans 8: 6KJV.

We exercise or make our human spirit

come alive by manifesting or responding to those desires birthed into our spirit by the working of God's power in us which include the desires to pray, fast, visit fellow Christians, evangelize, study God's word, bearing of spiritual fruits and so on.

I mean the surest way to exercise your spirit or make your spirit come alive is by focusing on the things of the Spirit.

"For they that are after the flesh do mind the things of the flesh; but they

that are after the spirit the things of the spirit."- Romans 8:5KJV

Furthermore, the power within us is made manifest in our lives for total transformation by our awareness and confessions. So then our source of power must come from our consciousness of this reality and our confessions. The consciousness alone is not enough, but it must go hand in hand with our confessions.

Romans 10:8-10KJV, "But what saith it? The word is nigh thee, even in thy mouth, and in thy heart: that is, the word of faith, which we preach; that is thou shalt confess with thy mouth the Lord Jesus, and shalt believe in thine heart that God hath raised him from the dead, thou shalt be saved. For with the heart man believeth unto righteousness; and with the mouth confession is made unto salvation."

Whatever it is we need or desire, we must first look within and acknowledge the truth that the Spirit of God in us is already doing that job.

Then we need to speak words like, *I declare the power of the Holy Spirit at work in me has caused me to possess all things that pertain to life and godliness for God has granted me including [name the specific area at this point] stability of health, financial breakthrough, grace, favour, boldness to preach the word of God, understanding of the deeper things of God, deliverance from all forms of satanic manipulations and oppressions in the Mighty name of Jesus Christ of Nazareth.*

This is how we live the life of dominion on earth. As He [Christ] is, so are we in this world (1 John 4:17). When we pray, we don't have to expect our answers to come from a God sitting on a glorious throne in heaven neither should we for a second think we don't have what we are asking for.

When Jesus taught the disciples to pray and believe that whatever they prayed for would be answered, it was right that time because the Holy Spirit as at that time hadn't come to make His permanent abode in them yet. Christ was still with them on earth. It was before Jesus was crucified and he arose from the dead. Now that the Holy Spirit has come to dwell in us, we need to grow in the things of God (1 Peter 2:2).

We are no longer to pray and expect to have answers from a God outside of ourselves sitting somewhere in the cosmos, but rather we must look on the inside of us to decree an answer to our prayers for the power at work in us is able to do more than we can think.

When ministers of the gospel shout *receive it, take it* and other stuffs like these, it is as though God has not deposited what they're declaring in the spirit of the members already. This is very dangerous. We as ministers should be very careful the way we present God to the church.

Moreover, there emerges another danger. It makes the members to yearn for something outside to come upon them whenever they are being ministered to. This can easily open great doors for demons to enter and operate. With time, the members simply lose focus of the tremendous power in them and begin to feel powerless and some kind of vulnerability.

Ministers of God are ordained by God to feed his flock. However, demonstration of the power of God does not come about all because a Man of God shouted take it, receive it and so on. The fact that it works for you doesn't mean it is in line with sound doctrine. God desires that we study to show ourselves approved.

As ministers we must learn, in our ministrations, to say things that agree with sound doctrine. Ponder over this and compare it with what some pastors often say and you would come to appreciate the difference.

By the mighty power of God at work in you as a child of God, I declare and decree the power is producing results for you in your finances, health, and marriage. Your womb is fertile and you're producing Godly children in the name of Jesus. It is evident now! You're manifesting what God has deposited in you in the mighty name of Jesus Christ of Nazareth. You're being made whole for greater is the one in you than he who is in the world. Glory to God!

CHAPTER 3

INSIGHT INTO PRAYER

"We are a new creation. We don't pray for daily provisions anymore. We simply manifest what God has excessively supplied us on a daily bases."- Rev. Foster Antwi

We don't receive answers to our prayers because we pray for long. Heartfelt, persistent, earnest and continued prayers don't grant us the answers to our prayers. We don't receive answers to our prayers because we know the best way to pray. Receiving answers have absolutely nothing to do with our efforts or what we put in. Answers to prayers do not come about as a result of our strict observance of the commandments of God. This doesn't mean that we are not to be doers of the word. In fact, spending more time crying and praying is completely out of the answer equation.

In the Old Testament, people received answers from God through these ways.

But in the New Testament, the formula has changed. The new creation man, created by the Word of God that lives and abides forever, receives answers from God because God has already accepted him in the Beloved and has made His abode in him. He simply delights in us!

Hebrews 2:11NLT, "So now Jesus and the ones he makes holy have the same Father. That is why Jesus is not ashamed to call them his brothers and sisters."

So we don't move God to minister to our needs by any of the formulas mentioned. His Spirit or the anointing at work in us ministers to our every need including those we don't even ask.

"For Christ is the end of the law for righteousness to every one that believeth." – Romans 10:4KJV

"Before they call I will answer, while they are yet speaking I will hear."- Isaiah 65:24NIV

"Likewise the Spirit helps us in our weak-

ness; for we do not know how to pray as we ought, but the Spirit himself intercedes for us with sighs too deep for words. And he who searches the hearts of men knows what is the mind of the Spirit, because the Spirit intercedes for the saints according to the will of God."-Romans 8:26-27RSV

The power of God in us works to produce diverse spiritual fruit and desires in us. One of such desires is prayer. No man can cultivate the Christian habit of prayer without the promptings of God. There are those whose prayer life is now comatose. It isn't that the power of God is not working to produce this desire in them but rather they allow themselves to be occupied by the things of this world. They do recognize their prayerlessness but they are some kind of too busy to pray. Others may even brood over it sometimes whenever the promptings come to them but would do nothing about it. Beloved if this is your situation I declare by the power of God Almighty at work in you that your prayer life is taking a new form in the name of Jesus Christ, Amen.

Prayer is meant to make our human spirit more receptive to the things of God. It opens up our spirit for us to receive deeper revelations and to understand divine mysteries.

Prayer gives the believer the strength to walk the Christian walk. There is a way the Christian should walk in this world. We are light to the world and salt on this earth. Above all, we are to bear the fruit of the Holy Spirit.

Ephesians 5:8NIV, "For you were once darkness, but now you are light in the Lord. Live as children of light."

Ephesians 5:15-17NIV, "Be very careful, then, how you live—not as unwise but as wise, making the most of every opportunity, because the days are evil. Therefore do not be foolish, but understand what the Lord's will is.

Matthew 5:13-16NIV

"You are the salt of the earth. But if the salt loses its saltiness, how can it be made salty again? It is no longer good

for anything, except to be thrown out and trampled underfoot. You are the light of the world. A town built on a hill cannot be hidden. Neither do people light a lamp and put it under a bowl. Instead they put it on its stand, and it gives light to everyone in the house. In the same way, let your light shine before others, that they may see your good deeds and glorify your Father in heaven."

The surest way we can overcome the schemes of the enemy in this life is by constant prayer. This is to say that, prayer shields us from all the attacks of the enemy. If prayer becomes part and parcel of our evangelism, the heart of unbelievers will be made soft and ready to receive the gospel and turn to Christ.

As you can see, prayer does a lot in the life of the believer. However, many are ignorant about the subject. Often people expect answers to their prayers to come from a God sitting on an exalted throne in heaven. The Bible makes it clear that this is not the case.

"Now ye are the body of Christ, and members in particular."- 1 Corinthians 12:27KJV.

"One God and Father of all, who is above all, and through all, and in you all." Ephesians 4:6KJV.

"But he that is joined unto the Lord is one spirit."- 1 Corinthians 6:17KJV

The truth is that, God is in us reconciling the world back to Himself. So when we pray, the answers to our prayers are released to our human spirit by the power of God working in us. It doesn't come from the outside of us but instead it happens on the inside of us.

It may seem nothing is happening when you look on the inside of you but I tell you the Spirit of God is at work in you. The Spirit of God which is the power of God dwelling in you is always receptive to your prayers. *Wherever the spirit of God goes, His presence, voice and power becomes more evident.*

The Spirit in us works through us like a river that flows to bring salvation to those afflicted by the devil. All that you need is to constantly activate the power in you so it would continue to flow. How do we activate the flow of God's power? Anything that acts as an impediment to the flow of that river or power should be removed. The impediment can come as a result of doubt, unbelief or lack of faith (Hebrews 11:6).

The same Spirit causes us to manifest the power of God in crusade grounds. One thing to enable you to distinguish this Holy Spirit from demonic operation is that it doesn't come upon you like a jacket, fire or electricity to cause you to heal the sick or cast out devils. Many men of God are quick to use these manifestations to conclude the power of God or the Holy Spirit has come upon them to perform mighty miracles.

The fact that you once experienced these manifestations and they worked for you doesn't mean that's how the Holy Spirit operates. Since these have been the consciousness of many men of God, their members also feel heat, cold or electricity during ministrations.

The signs mentioned above are the commonest ways to determine demonic spirit at work. The danger is if we don't study harder and understand how the Spirit of God operates, the tendency of we being used blindly by demons will be higher. This same thing happened to the Israelites. Study the account below:

"In the third year of Hoshea son of Elah, king of Israel, Hezekiah the son of Ahaz, king of Judah, began to reign. He was

twenty-five years old when he began to reign, and he reigned twenty-nine years in Jerusalem. His mother's name was Abi the daughter of Zechariah. And he did what was right in the eyes of the LORD, according to all that David his father had done. He removed the high places, and broke the pillars, and cut down the Asherah. And he broke in pieces the bronze serpent that Moses had made, for until those days the people of Israel had burned incense to it; it was called Nehustan. He trusted in the LORD the God of Israel; so that there was none like him among all the kings of Judah after him, nor among those who were before him. For he held fast to the LORD; he did not depart from following him, but kept the commandments which the LORD commanded Moses. And the LORD was with him; wherever he went forth, he prospered. He rebelled against the king of Assyria, and would not serve him."- 2 Kings 18:1-8RSV

As you can vividly see, they were blindly worshipping Satan by burning incense to the bronze serpent Moses made.

They secretly stole it on the desert and hid it from Moses (Numbers 21:5-10). I believe the devil caused the people to have diverse encounters and mind blowing testimonies after they hid it so the wrath of God would fall on them. Elijah came, he couldn't discern it. Elisha also operated in the anointing yet he also didn't notice it.

All the Judges of Israel after Joshua and good Kings like David and Jehoshaphat didn't see Satan was being worshipped through the bronze serpent.

This will never happen to you child of God. According to the Word of God, there is nothing greater and powerful than, 'Christ in you'. Let's be conscious of ourselves and desist from any form of mystical formulas believed to bring some kind of deliverance.

2 Corinthians 13:5KJV, ***"Examine yourselves, whether ye be in the faith;***

prove your own selves. Know ye not your own selves, how that Jesus Christ is in you, *except ye be reprobates?"*

The born again Christian, filled with the Holy Spirit of God, needs no deliverance again from the enemy. He is not under the curse of Adam. He is a new kind of being born by the Spirit of God. Those who have not confessed the Lord Jesus Christ as Lord and Saviour are still counted as part of this world and are under the complete manipulations of the devil. Those are still the descendants of the first Adam so Satan, the devil, has complete power over them. We have become the Sons of God. We are simply not part of this world so the systems of this world have no influence on the outcome of our lives irrespective of the hardships we go through, nothing can ever separate us from the love of God. (Read John Chapter 17)

John 1:10-13KJV, "He was in the world, and the world was made by him, and the world knew him not. He came unto his own, and his own received him not. But as many as received him, to them gave he power to become the sons of God, even to them that believe on his name: which were born, not of blood, nor of the will of the flesh, nor of the will of man, but of God."

CHAPTER 4

INSIGHT INTO FASTING

"Fasting is done not because we desperately need something from God but rather our heart is full of gratitude for what He has done for us. It should be a sign that the love of God is increasing in our hearts."- Rev. Foster Antwi

This is a very profound subject. Before we proceed there are basic things that we need to know about fasting. Fasting is simply abstaining from food for religious or medical reasons. For example, sick patients are required to fast before medical exam or surgery.

For the purpose of this work, let me explain the concept in a different way. Fasting can be explained as a deliberate attempt of turning yourself away from the delights of your flesh and fixing your gaze and wholesome attention onto God through heartfelt continued prayer for diverse encounters with Him for a stipulated time whether self-determined or divinely ordered.

Usually when one goes without food or water for a period of time or days, it is accounted as fasting. In *Acts 27:33KJV*, *we read, "And while the day was coming on, Paul besought them all to take meat, saying, this day is the fourteenth day that ye have tarried and continued fasting, having taken nothing."*

"In those days the multitude being very great, and having nothing to eat, Jesus called his disciples unto him, and saith unto them, I have compassion on the

multitude, because they have now been with me three days, and have nothing to eat: And if I send them away fasting to their own houses, they will faint by the way: for divers of them came from far."-Mark 8:1-3KJV

There are books that look deeper into the subject of fasting. This chapter will open you up to something that a lot of writers or Christians continue to miss about fasting and prayers.

Before I explain that to you, I want you to understand that God desires that His servant fast to seek His face. In the Bible, nations, groups of people and individuals had fasted. Even nations and individuals who were not from Israel also fasted and God answered them. God can call a whole nation to fast and seek His face.

When you read Joel 2:12-32, you would observe the following;

1. God is calling His people to fast. It isn't the Israelites deciding this fast but rather it is God Himself.

2. They are to seek His face with all their heart, and with fasting, weeping and mourning.

3. The fasting involves all the people including the elders, children, nursing infants, the poor, the rich, the widow and the orphan even the newly married or the bridegroom and his bride, no honeymoon for them.

4. The priests, the ministers of the LORD, are to weep and make intercessions with all their hearts between the porch and the altar.

5. There is a possibility of God hearing the cry of His people and bringing restoration.

6. Overflow of God's blessings as his people shall eat in plenty and be satisfied. This means there shall be no form of lack for God's people.

7. A promise of a massive outpouring of God's Spirit on all flesh likewise a supernatural deliverance for whoever calls on the name of the LORD.

Let's read what is recorded in *Joel 2:12-32KJV,* "*Therefore also now, saith the LORD, turn ye even to me with all your heart, and with fasting, and with weeping, and with mourning: and rend your heart, and not your garments, and turn unto the LORD your God: for he is gracious and merciful, slow to anger, and of great kindness, and repenteth him of the evil. Who knoweth if he will return and repent, and leave a blessing behind him; even a meat offering and a drink offering unto the LORD your God? Blow the trumpet in Zion, sanctify a fast, call a solemn assembly: Gather the people, sanctify the congregation, assemble the elders, gather the children, and those that suck the breasts: let the bridegroom go forth of his chamber, and the bride out of her closet. Let the priests, the ministers of the LORD, weep between the porch and the altar, and let them say, spare thy people, O LORD, and give not thine heritage to reproach, that the heathen should rule over them: wherefore should they say among the people, where is their God? Then will the LORD be jealous for his land, and pity his people. Yea, the LORD will answer and say unto his people, Behold, I will send you corn, and wine, and oil, and ye shall be satisfied therewith: and I will no more make you a reproach among the heathen: but I will remove far off from you the northern army, and will drive him into a land barren and desolate, with his face toward the east sea, and his hinder part toward the utmost sea, and his stink shall come up, and his ill savour shall come up, because he hath done great things. Fear not, O land: be glad and rejoice: for the LORD will do great things. Be not afraid, ye beasts of the field: for the pastures of the wilderness do spring, for the tree beareth her fruit, the fig tree and the vine do yield their strength. Be glad then, ye children of Zion, and rejoice in the LORD your God: for he hath given you the former rain moderately, and he will cause to come down for you the rain, the former rain, and the latter rain in the first month. And the floors shall be full of wheat, and the vats shall overflow with wine and oil. And I will restore to you the years that the locust hath eaten, the cankerworm, and the caterpiller, and the parlmerworm, my great army which I sent among you. And ye shall eat in plenty, and be satisfied, and praise the name of the LORD your God, that hath dealt wondrously with you: and my people shall never be ashamed. And ye shall know that I am in the midst of Israel, and that I am the LORD your God,* and none else: and my people shall never be ashamed. And it shall come to pass afterward, that I will pour out my spirit upon all flesh; and your sons and daughters shall prophesy, your old men shall dream dreams, your young men shall see visions: and also upon the servants and upon the handmaids in those days will I pour out my spirit. And I will shew wonders in the heavens and in the earth, blood, and fire, and pillars of smoke. The sun shall be turned into darkness, and the moon into blood, before the great and the terrible day of the LORD come. And it shall come to pass, that whosoever shall *call on the name of the LORD shall be delivered: for in mount Zion and in Jerusalem shall be deliverance, as the LORD hath said, and in the remnant whom the LORD shall call."*

On the contrary, a nation, isolated from God, also declared a fast to seek the face of God. A notable example in the Bible is what happened in Nineveh.

Jonah 3:1-10RSV, "Then the word of the LORD came to Jonah the second time, saying, "Arise, go to Nineveh, that great city and proclaim to it the message that I tell you." So Jonah arose and went to

Nineveh, according to the word of the LORD. Now Nineveh was an exceedingly great city, three days' journey in breadth. Jonah began to go into the city, going a day's journey. And he cried, "Yet forty days, and Nineveh shall be overthrown!" and the people of Nineveh believed God; they proclaimed a fast, and put on sackcloth, from the greatest of them to the least of them. Then tidings reached the king of Nineveh, and he arose from his throne, removed his robe, and covered himself with sackcloth, and sat in ashes. And he made proclamation and published through Nineveh, "By the decree of the king and his nobles: Let neither man nor beast, herd nor flock, taste anything; let them not feed, or drink water, but let man and beast be covered with sackcloth, and let them cry mightily to God; yea, let every one turn from his evil way and from the violence which is in his hands. Who knows, God may yet repent and turn from his fierce anger, so that we perish not?" when God saw what they did, how they turned from their evil way, God repented of the evil which he had said he would do to them; and he did not do it."

The fasting was a direct response to

what the Prophet of God proclaimed. In the case of Israel during the time of Nehemiah, they voluntarily fasted not in response to warnings from God's prophets but rather the awareness of their numerous transgressions. They therefore fasted to confess their sins and that of their fathers for God's unfailing mercy as recorded in Nehemiah Chapter 9. At the time the Israelites in exile faced danger of extinction under Haman, a fast was declared. (Study Esther Chapter 4)

In the Bible, groups of people fasted under God's instruction. Yet, other groups fasted voluntarily to provoke different encounters from God. Individual Israelite like Daniel fasted voluntarily. *"And I set my face unto the Lord God, to seek by prayer and supplications, with fasting, and sackcloth, and ashes".* *(Read Daniel Chapter 9)*

There were other Israelites who used fasting and prayers as service to God. At the time of Jesus Christ, the Bible confirms in *Luke 2:37KJV*, *"...a widow of about fourscore and four years, which departed not from the temple, but served God with fastings and prayers night and day.*

In the book of Acts Chapter 10, Cornelius, a Gentile, had this same attitude and God saved him and his entire household. In *Acts 10:30, 31KJV* we read, *"And Cornelius said, four days ago I was fasting until this hour; and at the ninth hour I prayed in my house, and , behold, a man stood before me in bright clothing, and said, Cornelius, thy prayer is heard, and thine alms are had in remembrance in the sight of God."*

I encourage you to make it a point to read the whole chapter of Acts 10 and continue to grow in your understanding of the things of God.

In the case of the disciples, fasting and prayers were done to ordain leaders for the church. *Acts 14:21-23KJV, "And when they had preached the gospel to that city, and had taught many, they returned again to Lystra, and to Iconium, and Antioch, confirming the souls of the disciples, and exhorting them to continue in the faith, and that we must through much tribulation enter into the kingdom of God. And when they had ordained them elders in every church, and hap prayed with fasting, they commended them to the Lord, on whom they believed."*

Fasting and prayers has so many spiritual benefits for the child of God. As much as God requires His servant to fast, He also expects them to cultivate the right attitude. Let's study *Isaiah Chapter 58:1-12KJV in bits, "Cry aloud, spare not, lift up your voice like a trum-*

pet; declare to my people their transgression, to the house of Jacob their sins. Yet they seek me daily, and delight to know my ways, as if they were a nation that did righteousness and did not forsake the ordinance of their God; they ask of me righteous judgments, they delight to draw near to God. 'Why have we fasted, and thou seest it not? Why have we humbled ourselves, and thou takest no knowledge of it?'

Fasting is a sign that one has humbled himself to seek the face of God. It is a way of telling God to take over since the strength, knowledge, wisdom and experience you've acquired cannot cause you to accomplish God's purposes for your life.

God was not pleased at all with the Israelites. They didn't follow the ordinances of God neither did they seek after righteousness. They were living for themselves and with that there was no way their voices could be heard from on high. No one had compassion for the poor and needy. The naked in the midst of them were not clothed. Wickedness filled their hearts so much to the extent that they turned their backs against their kinsmen. God therefore refused to answer them in the day of distress.

"Behold, in the day of your fast you seek your own pleasure, and oppress all your workers. Behold, you fast only to quarrel and to fight and to hit with wicked fist. Fasting like yours this day will not make your voice to be heard on high. Is such the fast that I choose, a day for a man to humble himself? Is it to bow down his head like a rush, and to spread sackcloth and ashes under him? Will you call this a

fast, and a day acceptable to the LORD?"

God through His Prophet Isaiah began to point exactly where the people had missed the mark and to call them unto repentance. Isaiah revealed to them how God expected them to live on daily bases. They are the things that move God to intervene in the affairs of His people.

"Is not this the fast that I choose: to loose the bonds of wickedness, to undo the thongs of the yoke, to let the oppressed go free, and to break every yoke? Is it not to

share your bread with the hungry, and bring the homeless poor into your house; when you see the naked, to cover him, and not to hide yourself from your own flesh?"

Those who live by this truth have everlasting rewards to receive from God at the second coming of Christ. *"When the Son of man comes in his glory, and all the angels with him, then he will sit on his glorious throne. Before him will be gathered all the nations, and he will separate them one from another as a shepherd separates the sheep from the goats, and he will place the sheep at his right hand, but the goats at the left. Then the King will say to those at his right hand, 'Come, O blessed of my Father, inherit the kingdom prepared for you from the foundation of the world; for I was hungry and you gave me food, I was thirsty and you gave me drink, I was a stranger and you welcomed me, I was naked and you clothed me, I was sick and you visited me, I was in prison and you came to me.' Then the righteous will answer him, 'Lord, when did we see thee hungry and feed thee, or thirsty and give thee drink? And when did we see thee a stranger and welcome thee, or naked and clothe thee? And when did we see thee sick or in prison and visit thee? And the King will answer them, 'Truly, I say to you, as you did it to one of the least of these my brethren, you did it for me.'"- Mathew 25:31-40KJV*

The Israelites were seeking for something they could have readily enjoyed in this life if they had lived accordingly. Let's see some of the immediate benefits they could have enjoyed.

"Then shall your light break forth like

the dawn, and your healing shall spring up speedily; your righteousness shall go before you, the glory of the LORD shall be your rear guard. Then you shall call, and the LORD will answer; you shall cry, and he will say, Here I am. If you take away from the midst of you the yoke, the pointing of the finger, and speaking wickedness, if you pour yourself out for the hungry and satisfy the desire of the afflicted, then shall your light rise in the darkness and your gloom be as the noonday. And the LORD will guide you continually, and satisfy your desire with good things, and make your bones strong; and you shall be like a watered garden, like a spring of water, whose waters fail not. And your ancient ruins shall be rebuilt; you shall be called the repairer of the breach, the restorer of streets to dwell in."

I have been attending Atwea Mountains in the Ashanti Region of Ghana for prayers since 2010. Usually, I would make a long list of prayer requests of other people and would climb the mountains to pray. On the mountains, we mean serious business. People from all walks of life and of varying ages do come and pray. The weather can be extremely cold at Camp 3, the Methodist Camp. Sometimes when all the rooms are full, I sleep on the rocks. Aside the unfavourable weather conditions I endure, the cost of living on the mountains is very expensive. Despite all these challenges, thousands of people climb the mountain for an encounter with God.

Travelling from Koforidua all the way to the Atwea Mountains has become a part and parcel of me. There is always a blessing when one isolates himself from relatives and friends to *seek the face of God* ***[We no longer seek the face of God when we confess Jesus Christ as our Lord and Saviour. This is because; God comes to make His abode in us. Wherever we go God goes. We simply become the face of God]***. I believe there are spiritual keys released as one goes to the mountains to pray when such opportunity is available.

God has been so good to me. He has always answered my prayers and given numerous minds blowing and mind boggling testimonies to all those I stand to intercede for.

Something happened to me when I visited the mountains in December 2018. In the middle of the prayers, God spoke to me. He opened the eyes of my understanding and taught me mysteries which propelled the writing of this book.

Many might think they are well versed in the word of God but their confessions and the kind of things they say prove otherwise. I know God is doing a new thing in our lives. For whenever God is about to do something new, He first of all will cause your eyes of understanding to be enlightened. Then God will begin to open up to you divine mysteries.

To start with, we don't fast to tell God to grant us certain things we need for God has already met our needs. ***Fasting is done not because we desperately need something from God but rather our heart is full of gratitude for what He has done for us. It should be a sign that the love of God is increasing in our***

hearts.

The point of fasting and prayers is no longer, *"ask, and it will be given you; seek, and you will find; knock, and it will be opened to you."- Matthew 7:7NIV*

Observe the tenses used and you would realize that the construction is in the future tense. Notice that Jesus Christ said this before the outpouring of the Holy Spirit on the day of Pentecost in Acts Chapter 2.

When the Holy Spirit came upon us to make His abode in us, the formula has changed. *"His divine power has granted to us all things that pertain to life and godliness, through the knowledge of him who called us to his own glory and excellence"- 2 Peter 1:3RSVA.* Now, we express our faith in God's word by thanking God for granting us all that we need. We don't go like 'God I need healing', 'God I need financial break-through' and 'God bring me a spouse'.

Any prayer you pray requesting God to do something for you simply means you're not growing in your faith and in your knowledge of Christ. What you need to say is, "God thank you so much for your healing power is at work in me. That power functioning in me makes me healthy in my bones, blood and cells in the name of Jesus Christ of Nazareth." That's how you need to talk.

If you are a minister of the Gospel, help the Body of Christ to grow in the things of God by refusing to shout *receive it*; *take it*, and so on. Help them to come to the consciousness of what God has granted them and let them exercise their faith in it. This way, they would live a life of dominion here on earth.

The point of fasting is no longer to plead for forgiveness for your numerous transgressions. In Christ, we are forgiven, sanctified and justified. There is no condemnation for those in Christ Jesus. Fast out of gratitude to God for accomplishing what you could never have attained by your own accord.

Also, fasting is not done to find out God's mind about a decision you need to make in life for Christ has become our wisdom. His Spirit moves us to always make the right decisions. As we abide in Him and He in us, we can never be disadvantaged. All things work together for our good because we love God. This therefore means that our decisions and choices in life are propelled by the Spirit of God for the Word of God dwells in us richly. Our fasting should simply be praises to God because His profound wisdom is working in us causing us to live triumphantly in this life.

Moreover, there are other ministers of the Gospel who are of the view that fasting is important to empower us cast devils and heal the sick. They affirm that even with what Jesus Christ Himself said recorded in *Mark 9:29KJV*, *"And he said unto them, this kind can come forth by nothing, but by prayer and fasting." [Also Matthew 17:21]*

Jesus indeed said this but it was before His crucifixion and ascension to heaven. The Bible clearly tells us that Satan was completely defeated when Jesus died on the cross. *"In this way, he disarmed the spiritual rulers and authorities. He shamed them publicly by his victory over them on the cross"*- Colos-

sians 2:15NLT. We have been placed in the realm of power above Satan and all his cohorts of demons. *"And God raised us up with Christ and seated us with him in the heavenly realms in Christ Jesus."-Ephesians 2:6NIV*

Understanding what the cross and the blood of Jesus accomplished for you would cause you to deal with the enemy with ease without any form of pressure. Affirm what God has accomplished for you and base on that to minister grace to all those held captive by the enemy.

Don't fast to fight Satan and his demons again. Simply put them where they belong, in total defeat and failure. Fast with praises to God for defeating such a formidable foe for you to triumph in life!

CHAPTER 5

Dominate Your World

"The fact that you used the handkerchief and the apple and you got your healing doesn't mean it came from God. You can get diverse testimonies by applying mystical formulas but in the end, when God looks at you and you don't have the Spirit of Christ in you, you are simply none of His. It doesn't worth it to exchange your soul with the enemy for breakthroughs in

*this life only to lose your soul in the end."-
Rev. Foster Antwi*

The Bible recounts that the Israelites were into idolatry. They didn't walk in the statutes of God neither did they respect God's holy prophets at the time of King Ahab.

Elijah grieved in his heart and sought for every avenue to turn the people back to Jehovah. To prove that Jehovah is the Sovereign Lord and the Lord of Hosts and that he was His mouthpiece on earth, Elijah decreed and God honoured his word.

1 Kings 17:1KJV, "And Elijah the Tishbite, who was of the inhabitants of Gilead, said unto Ahab, as the LORD God of Israel liveth, before whom I stand, there shall not be dew nor rain these years, but according to my word."

James 5:17KJV, "Elias was a man subject to like passions as we are, and he prayed earnestly that it might not rain: and it rained not on the earth by the space of three years and six months."

One thing about Elijah was that, when he made that statement, he knew he would also be terribly affected in a way but then since it had to do with honouring Jehovah, he went forward to declare with the authority in the name of Jehovah.

This was a man who was very eager to go the extra mile to see the will and purpose of God established in Israel. The spiritual welfare of his people was his ultimate concern.

In life, we would encounter so many things that will bring frustrations and disappointment. Things may not always be the way we want it to be. But if we sincerely want to change things to glorify God, we must be ever willing to pay the price.

I know so many students and university graduates whose lives seem miserable in the eyes of some of their mates simply because they are not willing to follow the crowd to commit some serious sins that are deemed as normal by those who have no reverential fear for God. They detest and shun any 'get-rich quick' methods so they don't stake neither do they engage in lotto, sports bet, internet fraud, gay and lesbianism, prostitution likewise bribery and corruption at work places. They may seem as people wallowing in poverty by their colleagues but in the end, it is always a blessing because the paths of a just man are ordered by God.

Exodus 23:2NIV, "Do not follow the crowd in doing wrong. When you give testimony in a lawsuit, do not pervert justice by siding with the crowd."

Psalm 37:16, "A little that a righteous man hath is better than the riches of many wicked."

Proverbs 14:12, "There is a way which seemeth right unto a man, but the end thereof are the ways of death."

Proverbs 12:2,3, "A good man obtaineth favour of the LORD: but a man of wicked devices will he condemn. A man shall not be established by wickedness: but the root of the righteous shall not be moved."

There are some beautiful Christian ladies who haven't been able to locate their soul mates and are still single because they have purposed deep in their hearts never to compromise their faith. They are never ready to break their virginity to prove they love the men that come their way. These ladies are often ridiculed and are given all sorts of names. However, they rejoice exceedingly in the end.

Luke 6:22KJV, "Blessed are ye, when men shall hate you, and when they shall separate you from their company, and shall reproach you, and cast out your name as evil, for the Son of man's sake."

Beloved reader, understand that if you want to enforce God's divine purpose here on earth, you would have to develop a strong heart and an uncompromising faith like Daniel and his three friends (Daniel 3:16-18). Your business may frown at you. You may even be unemployed despite hundreds of applications submitted and countless interviews you might have attended. A lot of Christian ladies are unemployed because they hesitated to have any unhealthy affair with the male employers.

Yours may even be sickness you're struggling to get healed. Like the woman with the issue of blood, you too might have spent your last 'pesewa' (coin) on healers and doctors alike but the story still seem the same (Mark 5:24-29). Nothing good seems to come out from your toil. With this very condition, it is not uncommon for you to hear voices telling you what to do. People you didn't even invite to comment about your predicaments would begin to offer you a solution by convincing you on why you should contact that native doctor and why you should even join the secret society.

The story seems endless. However, irrespective of what you may be facing, understand that God has something to say about it. If you don't know, God has already spoken that His plans for us are not of evil but of good to give us an expected end (Jeremiah 29:11). That expected end is found in Jesus Christ, our Saviour. It is only in Christ Jesus that we can enjoy the totality of God's promises and power. All the promises of God are made complete in Christ Jesus. In other words, anything God has promised His sons in the word are obtainable only in Christ Jesus. Jesus Christ is therefore the fullness of God's promises.

2 Corinthians 1:19-20KJV, "For the Son of God, Jesus Christ, who was preached among you by us, even by me and Silvanus and Timotheus, was not yea and nay, but in him was yea. For all the promises of God in him are yea, and in him Amen, unto the glory of God by us". So when you come to Christ, you're divinely mandated to be partakers of the inheritance of the saints. (Colossians 1:12)

We should boldly declare what we know God has said concerning the challenges confronting us to quench the fiery darts of the enemy otherwise we can't glorify our maker. Search the scriptures to find out what God has said concerning your case and build your faith on them. Speak words that are in consonant with what God says concerning that situation.

You have to get to the level where you are not perturbed by the storms of life.

Get to that level where the only thing you can ever say is what God says concerning your situation and not the fleeting pain you feel in your body.

Elijah spoke to King Ahab as a result of the unwavering faith he had in Jehovah and he had no time to consider or worry whether God would honour the word he had spoken or not. Elijah knew one thing for sure, that God would never let him down or put him to shame no matter what.

Remember, Elijah's encounter with King Ahab and the conversation that ensued that very day were all re-corded by the King's scribe. None of these frightened the Prophet of God. He looked beyond the physical, what people would say should his word proved false, and been filled with the Spirit of the living God, he let out the message that would drastically change the economic situation that time. Truly, Elijah looked beyond self-gratification and never bothered about his survival afterwards. All that he was concerned about was the God of Israel being vindicated as the one and only true God and not Baal.

As you make it a point to speak faith filled words into every aspect of your life, it is important not to focus on what other people would say. There are those who would think you're boasting too much. Brother, remember you cannot be understood. You're a new creature created by the incorruptible word of God. You dwell in the city of the Most High God.

Hebrews 12:22-24KJV, "But ye are come unto mount Sion, and unto the city of the living God, the heavenly Jerusalem, and to an innumerable company of angels, to the general assembly and church of the firstborn, which are written in heaven, and to God the judge of all, and to the spirits of just men made perfect, and to Jesus the mediator of the new covenant, and to the blood of sprinkling, that speaketh better things than that of Abel."

That's your abode, you don't belong here. Your fellowship is not with worldly men but your fellowship is with God and His Son Jesus Christ.

1 John 1:3,4KJV, "That which we have

seen and heard declare we unto you, that ye also may have fellowship with us: and truly our fellowship is with the Father, and with his Son Jesus Christ. And these things write we unto you, that your joy may be full."

Keep saying what the word of God says about you. Claim all the promises of God to yourself and it wouldn't be long you will begin to witness the manifestations of whatever word you speak. This is what makes us partakers of God's divine nature (2 Peter1:3, 4). We effect changes with our confessions.

Glory to God!

Elijah never gave thought to himself. He was only concerned about proving the power of God and turning his generation away from idol worship. We must live not for ourselves but for our maker and constantly seek His interests.

God is raising people in this generation to stand for Him like the Prophet Elijah to boldly declare the word of God in season without compromise whatsoever. It is time for you to see beyond the self and to enforce God's overall purpose for mankind at every point in life.

The power of God at work in us makes us enforcers of God's salvation plan. Remember the word of God says that God is in us to reconcile the world back to Himself. This is our divine assignment. Irrespective of where we find ourselves and the kind of work we are engaged in, God wants to see us employing every avenue to spread His salvation message. You may even have some friends on social media platforms that are not born again Christians. Allow yourself for God to reach them through you. People need to hear about this new life.

Acts 5:20KJV, "Go, stand and speak in the temple to the people all the words of this life."

We are divine enforcers of God's purposes on earth. Recognize what you carry and begin to speak faith-filled words to change every situation that is contrary to God's will. Remember, Elijah had no time to resort to oil, handkerchief, apple, salt, sticker, calendar or any honey direction as we see practiced by some ministers of the gospel. Even though you may be divinely instructed, those are only temporary and they bring short term relieve. God's purpose is for us to know He has resided in us and has deposited His power in us which is constantly at work in us. It is that same power that raised Jesus from the dead. Miracles, signs and wonders can happen without resulting to any mystical formulas. When Jesus sent His disciples, they went about proclaiming repentance of sins and mighty miracles, signs and wonders happened at the mention of the name Jesus. They didn't use any of the anointed materials sold and used in today's churches.

Satan seeks to take dominion over the children of God simply because many of us are ignorant of God's word. Constant application of mystical formulas has led many into spiritual captivity. *The fact that you used the handkerchief and the apple and you got your healing doesn't mean it came from God. You can get diverse testimonies by applying mystical formulas but in the end, when God looks at you and you don't have the Spirit of Christ in you, you are simply none of His. It doesn't worth it to exchange your soul with the enemy for breakthroughs in this life only to lose your soul in the end.* Ponder over this scripture;

Romans 8:5-9ESV, "For those who live according to the flesh set their minds on the things of the flesh, but those who live according to the Spirit set their minds on the things of the Spirit. To set the mind on the flesh is death, but to set the mind on the Spirit is life and peace. For the mind that is set on the flesh is hostile to God;

it does not submit to God's law, indeed it cannot; and those who are in the flesh cannot please God. But you are not in the flesh, you are in the Spirit, if in fact the Spirit of God dwells in you. Any one who does not have the Spirit of Christ does not belong to him."

As you can see, we live in the spirit and operate there. That is why we need to set our affection on the things of the Spirit and not on the things of the flesh. Sprinkling all kinds of oil in our rooms and anointing even our cars with oil is not how we live in the spirit. There are those who go for baths from some ministers of God for spiritual cleansing to get visas and receive favours from those in high authority. Some people even bath with some leaves believed to possess the powers to ward off evil and terminate all demonic activities. All these directions are given to them by their pastors. What's the difference between the native doctor and the man of God that practices these things?

There is power inside of you. The same power that raised Christ from the dead is at work in you. Acknowledge what is inside of you and begin to release the power inside of you to effect changes in your world and circumstances. We walk in authority and dominion by speaking words of faith in line with the revelation of the new creation man. When I say the revelation of the new creation man, I mean what we have become in Christ. If you keep silent, the enemy will override you. Don't give place to the devil! Declare your rights as a child of God and walk in dominion.

See, the power inside of you do not increase or decrease. This is so because,

God does not increase or decrease in power. He is the full embodiment of Power. He neither increase in wisdom nor decrease in wisdom for He is wisdom itself. The amazing thing is that, you have the anointing of God without measure for Christ has come to make His permanent abode in you. You don't need to be ordained as a minister before you get the anointing of God. You cannot receive the Holy Spirit by the laying on of hands by a highly anointed man of God. That will only bring demons into you to tell you the truth. The Holy Spirit comes into you the very moment you confess Christ as Lord and Saviour. As you grow in your knowledge of God, you will learn to talk differently, you will speak faith-filled words that will make the power of God resident in you more of a reality in your life through daily confessions. Now what's the point of ordination? When a person is anointed with oil and ordained into the ministry, the purpose is to set him apart from the masses and to officially commission him to commence the work of the ministry. He is then identified and accepted as a person with divine assignment and mission

(Numbers 8:9-26, 25:15-22 and Deuteronomy 34:9).

1 Timothy 4: 14, "Neglect not the gift that is in thee, which was given thee by prophecy, with the laying on of the hands of the presbytery."

The laying on of hands received doesn't transfer any power directly from those that lay the hands. Any transfer of spiritual ability, grace and power is done by the will of God and not the individual ministers laying the hands.

"It is the one and only Spirit who distributes all these gifts. He alone decides which gift each person should have."- 1 Corinthians 12:11NLT.

Moreover, the person to be ordained is already born again and he or she might even be operating mightily in the power of God before the ordination. So then the laying on of hands activates his human spirit to be more conscious of the voice of the Spirit as he is about to walk on new spiritual grounds he has never walked before. In other sense, his human spirit becomes more receptive to the things of God so he can from that time onwards walk in the sensitivity of the power of God and in the fullness of the Holy Ghost. He receives boldness to preach the Gospel. This was exactly what happened to Peter. (Read Acts 4:8-12, and Acts Chapter 2)

CHAPTER 6

THE MOMENT OF SALVATION

Beloved, at this point I want you to know what happens to the believer at the point of salvation. I encourage you to study them continuously so you can walk in dominion here on earth.

It is only in Christ Jesus that we have such an inheritance. No other god in other religions can grant us these things that I am about to share with you from the Word of God.

After you've gone through all the Bible references I have provided, the enemy would no longer claim ownership over you since you will discover your rights as a child of God. You wouldn't be chasing for any mystical formulas or directions from anywhere for wealth, protection or favour.

Satan and his cohorts of demons are limited in powers so much that those who worship them are pretty well aware the very reason they have different demons for diverse activities. Their believers worship demons in the air, sun, moon, stars, and planets like Jupiter, Saturn, Mars and Venus are all worshipped. Some even continue to worship thunder, demons in plants, mountains, rivers and the oceans. As if that was all, people have demons they consult before beginning any venture like crop planting, harvesting, marriage, childbirth and travelling. People still worship animals and do carry charms and amulets on them wher-

ever they go for numerous purposes.
When situations become unbearable
for them, they invoke the spirit of their
dead ancestors through the pouring of
libation to seek assistance. What a life
of slavery!

Kindly take your Bible and let's go
through these scriptures together.
It is time for us to discover what
God has done for us and what
we have become in Him.

What God has done – who we are

1. He foreknew us – Rom 8:29, 1 Pet 1:2

2. He elected us – Rom 8:33, Col 3:12, 1Thes 1:4, Tit 1:1, 1 Pet 1:2

3. He predestinated us – Rom 8:29,30; Eph 1:5, 11

4. We are chosen – Mat 22:14, 1 Pet 2:4

5. We are called – 1 Thes 5:24

6. We are reconciled by God – 2 Cor 5:18-19; Col 1:20

7. We are reconciled to God – Rom 5:10; 2 Cor 5:20

8.   Redeemed by God – Rom 3:24; Col 1:14; 1 Pet 1:18

9.   We are born again spiritually – Jn 3:7; 1 Pet 1:23

10.   We are regenerated – Jn 13:10; 1 Cor 6:11; Titus 3:5

11.   We are made righteous and the righteousness of God is unto us and upon us who believe – Rom 3:22; 1 Cor 1:30; 2 Cor 5:21; Gal 3:22, Phil 3:9

12.   We are justified – Acts 13:39; Rom 3:26, 5:1, 8:30; 1 Cor 6:11; Titus 3:7

13.   We are glorified – Rom 8:30

14.   We receive the Spirit of adoption – Rom 8:15-16,23; Gal

4:4-6, God is our Father 1 Cor 1:3;

8:6; Gal 1:4; Eph 1:2; 4:6

15.   We are complete in Him – Col 2:10

16.   We are sanctified – 1

Cor 1:30, 6:11

17.   Forgiven – Acts 10:43; Rom

4:25; Col 1:14; 2:13; 3:13; Eph

1:7; 4:32; 1 Pet 2:24

18.   Quickened, brought to life –

Rom 4:17, Eph 2:1; Col 2:13.

19.   Perfected forever – Heb 10:14

20.   We are accepted – Eph

1:6; 1 Pet 2:5

21.   We are made meet – Col 1:12

22.	We are crucified with Christ –

Rom 6:6, 6:8; Gal 2:20; 1 Pet 2:24

23.	Buried with Christ –

Rom 6:4; Col 2:12

24.	We are born of the Spirit – Jn 3:6

27.	We are baptized with the

Spirit – 1 Cor 12:13; 10:17

28.	We have the earnest, or deposit,

of the Holy Spirit, securing our place in

heaven – 2 Cor 1:22; 5:5; Eph 1:13,14

29.	Indwelt by the Spirit – Jn

7:39; Rom 5:5, 8:9; 1 Cor 6:19;

2 Cor 1:22; Gal 4:6

30.	We are in God – 1 Thes 1:1

31.   We are in Christ – Jn 14:20

32.   We are in the Spirit – Rom 8:9

34.   We are dead to the law – Rom 7:4

35.   We are delivered from the law –

Rom 6:14, 7:6; 2 Cor 3:11; Gal 3:25

36.   We are circumcised in

Christ – Rom 2:29

37.   Made near to God by the blood

of Christ – Eph 2:13, 2:13-15

38.   We are delivered from the power

of darkness – Col 1:13, 2:13-15

39.   We are translated into the

Kingdom of God's dear Son – Col 1:13

40.   We are given as a gift to Christ by the Father – Jn 17:6,11,12,20; 10:29

41.   He gives us life in His name – Jn 20:31 and eternal life in His Son. Jn 3:15-16, 36; 5:24; 6:47; 11:25; 1 Jn 5:11-12

42.   We will never die – Jn 11:26

What He (Christ) is to the Believer

43.   Jesus Christ is our propitiation – Rom 3:25,26; 1 Jn 2:2

44.   Jesus Christ is our foundation – Eph 2:20; 1 Cor 3:11; 2 Cor 1:21

45.   Jesus Christ is our life – Col 3:4

46.   He is our Head – Col 2:10

47.   Our husband – 2 Cor 11:2

48.   He is our advocate – 1 Jn 2:1

49.   He is our brother – Heb 2:11

50.   He is our friend – Jn 15:15

51.   Our Shepherd -   Jn 10:11; 1 Pet 2:25

52.   Our high priest – Heb 3:1; 4:14; 6:20

What He makes us

53.   Sons of God – 2 Cor 6:18; Gal 3:26; 1 Jn 3:2 and children of God – Rom 9:26

54.   A new creation – 2 Cor 5:17; Gal 6:15

55.   Members of His Body – 1 Cor 12:13

56.   His bride – Eph 5:25-27

57.   Saints – 1Cor 1:2

58.   His holy priesthood – 1 Pet 2:5,9 and his royal priesthood – 1 Pet 2:9; Rev 1:6

59.   A chosen generation, a peculiar people – Tit 2:14; 1 Pet 2:9

60.   His inheritance – Eph 1:18

61.   God's building – 1 Cor 3:9; our body is His temple – 1 Cor 3:16, 6:19

62.   Heavenly citizens – Luke 10:20; Eph 2:19; Phil 3:20; Heb 12:22

63.   Labourers together with Him – 1 Cor 3:9, 2 Cor 6:1

64.   Ambassadors for Christ – 2 Cor 5:20

65.   Ministers of God – 2 Cor 3:3, 6; 6:4

66.   His household – Gal 6:10; Eph 2:19

67.   His people – 2 Cor 6:16

68.   His beloved –Rom 9:25

What we have

69.   There is no condemnation for the believer – Rom 8:1; Jn 3:18, 5:24; 1 Cor 11:32

70.   We reign in life as more than conquerors – Rom 5:17; 8:37

71.   Light in the Lord – Eph 5:8; 1 Thes 5:4

72.   We have access to God – Rom 5:2; Eph 2:18; Heb 4:14-16; Heb 10:19-20

73.   He loves us – Jn 3:16; Eph 2:4, 5:2

74.   He gives us His grace – Eph 2:8

75.   He gives us His power –

Eph 1:19, Phil 2:13

76.   He is faithful to us –

Phil 1:6; Heb 13:5

77.   He gives us His peace – Col 3:15

78.   He gives us hope – Eph 1:18

79.   He gives us every spiritual

blessing – Eph 1:3

80.   He gives us rest – Heb

4:3, Mat 11:28

81.   He gives us joy – Rom

15:13; 1 Pet 1:8

82.   He consoles us – 2 Thes 2:16

83. He intercedes for us – Heb 7:25, 9:24; Rom 8:34

84. He keeps us – Rom 5:2

85. He instructs us – Tit 2:12,13

86. He saves us in the details and circumstances of life – Rom 1:16

87. He gives us an inheritance – Eph 1:14; Col 3:24; Heb 9:15; 1 Pet 1:4

88. We have fellowship with Him – 1 Cor 1:9; 1 Jn 1:9

89. He is faithful to us in suffering – Rom 8:18; Phil 1:29; Col 1:24; 1 Thes 3:3; 2 Tim 2:12; 1 Pet 2:20, 4:12

90.   The Word of God works in us – 1 Thes 2;13

91.   We are not ashamed – Rom 9:33, 10:11

92.   We will never thirst again – Jn 6:35

93.   We will not be confounded – 1 Pet 2:6

94.   We overcome the world – 1 Jn 5:5

95.   His great power is toward us who believe – Eph 1:19.

Beloved, having identified what God has done for us and what He has made us, we need to affirm our faith in whatever God says concerning us.

In the next chapter which is the last chapter of this book, I have given you some confessions and affirmations you need to swallow into your spirit to manifest whatever God has given you. The confessions and affirmations will cause you to walk in dominion here on earth. There are those who confess that life is full of ups and downs. This is not your portion beloved reader. Keep saying what God has done for you and see your life move forwards and upwards.

Hallelujah!

CHAPTER 7

CONFESSIONS AND AFFIRMATIONS

"Render the forces of darkness and their operations on unbelievers ineffective by your daily confessions"-Rev. Foster Antwi

I am the effulgence of God's Glory. I carry God's power to create wealth for my generations therefore I influence my world with divine power of God and cause positive change in every circumstances of life.

Christ has been made wisdom unto me and His divine revelation is functioning in me therefore I have perfect understanding to deal with the issues of life. God has given me the ability to apply specific and exact mysteries from God's word to every issue. My choice and decisions are faultless and deeply rooted in the wisdom of God.

I am a victor in Christ Jesus. All things are working together for my good. My faith filled words are producing great results everywhere I go. I am getting stronger by the day, every cell of my blood, bone and fibre of my being is energized by the same Spirit that raised Jesus from the dead.

I refuse to struggle in life. I declare that the lines have fallen unto me in pleasant places and I have a goodly heritage. All things are working together for my good. I do not look into visible things that are temporal but I keep my eyes on Jesus, the author and finisher of my faith for in Christ Jesus is the hope of my glory.

The anointing of God's Spirit is residing in every member of my family, and I declare in the name of God Almighty that every one of my family is working in the abundant grace of God causing them to prosper in all things.

The grace of God that brings salvation to all men has appeared to everyone in my family. That grace has brought divine health, peace, joy, progress and prosperity to rest upon every member of my family and it causes us to be fruitful and productive in every area of our lives.

I am fully resolved to maintain constant fellowship with my Father through prayer. I declare that each time of communion is an opportunity for me to be transformed to a higher realm of divine possibilities. My relationship with God results in the transformation of my mind, thought, words, love and passion for the unsaved. Therefore as I pronounce words of faith in prayer, tremendous power is released to effect the changes I desire. Each time I pray, I set up a mighty force that put the devil and the cohorts of hell into flight.

Today I step out by faith in the word of God and I take complete possession of everything that's rightfully mine in Christ Jesus. He has brought me into a place of indescribable wealth and health and I remain fruitful and productive because of the indwelling presence of His Spirit.

I affirm that I shine in my finances. God has opened unto me new channels of opportunities and blessings. Money comes unto me by free course in increasing measure, through multiple streams of income on a continuous basis. I am lavishly supplied. For out of God's fullness and abundance I have received and I am supplied with one grace after another and spiritual blessing upon spiritual blessing, even favour upon favour and gift heaped upon gift. For I know the grace of my Lord Jesus, that though he was rich, yet for my sake he became poor that I through his poverty may be rich. I am so rich, I am conscious of my wealth and riches in Christ. All things are working together for my good. I can never be disadvantaged, all things are working together to favour my cause. God has freely given me all things to enjoy. I am living in abundance. Glory to God!

Thank you Lord Jesus for your Word imparts wisdom to my spirit. It gives me a mind-set for success, victory, and dominion. I deal excellently in all my affairs of life and make accurate judgments and decisions because of your wisdom that propels me from within. I am in Christ; I am far removed from poverty, sickness, death, defeat, destruction, and failure. The eyes of my understanding are enlightened, therefore, I see the invisible and I am empowered to do the impossible. I declare that situations that are not consistent with your perfect will for my life are overturned and the works of the devil are frustrated in and around me, in the name of Jesus.

I affirm that I am a legal representative of the heavenly Kingdom, called and separated from the world. I am from above; therefore, I am not subject to the distracting elements and corrupting influences of this world. I belong in God's Kingdom, where I enjoy the full blessings and privileges of my kingdom inheritance. I am an offspring of the light; my whole being is full of light. I've been granted the Word and the Holy Spirit to help me become a more effective minister of the Gospel, having greater influence, reach and impact in the world today. I am divinely positioned as the light and hope of an ailing world! Through me, the unsaved in my world hear and receive the light of the Gospel, and are transformed and turned from darkness to light, and from the power of Satan unto God. I am abundantly supplied and furnished to send the Gospel into the nations of the world, so that more souls will be ushered into the Kingdom. Daily, I walk in the light; I refuse to be quiet about the Gospel, for it is the power of God unto salvation. That power is released to turn men from darkness to light and from the power of Satan unto God as I proclaim the Gospel today. Blessed be God. Hallelujah!

www.ingramcontent.com/pod-product-compliance
Lightning Source LLC
Chambersburg PA
CBHW020340160726
47992CB00004B/1904